SERMON FOR THE CRISIS.

DELIVERED BEFORE THE

ISSIONARY SOCIETY

OF THE

Detroit Annual Conference

OF THE M. E. CHURCH,

AT SAGINAW CITY, SEPTEMBER 6, 1867.

BY

REV. J. S. SMART.

DETROIT:
PUBLISHED BY J. M. ARNOLD & CO.
Wm. Graham's Steam Presses.
1867.

PREFACE.

The following discourse was written for my own congregation in Ypsilanti, Michigan, without any thought of publication. Being appointed to deliver the Annual Missionary Sermon before the Detroit Conference, I repeated it there, and the audience demanded it for publication. This demand, which I could not resist, is my apology for allowing it to be printed. Could I print the heart-throbs which accompanied its composition and delivery, and beget in others the deep solicitude I have felt for the conversion of the world, its publication would afford me the highest pleasure. But what I have felt in view of the decline in our missionary efforts, in this Conference, cannot be printed.

I am positive that very much more good can be done by the delivery of such a sermon as this, than any ordinary reader would derive from a printed copy. If, therefore, any of my brethren desire me to preach upon the subject in their pulpits during the current year, I will do so as far as practicable.

I feel that the present is an emergency which calls for special effort in behalf of our missionary work, and this conviction induces me to make this tender of my services. We have certainly come to a CRISIS in our missionary affairs. We cannot go back; we must go forward, or betray the cause of Christ.

J. S. S.

SERMON.

"*I am debtor both to the Greeks, and to the Barbarians; both to the wise, and to the unwise.*

So, as much as in me is, I am ready to preach the Gospel to you that are at Rome also."—ROMANS.—1. 14–15.

The worst man in the world is he that hath no place in his heart for any being but himself, and the best men are they who have room in their hearts for all mankind. Such a man was Paul. He sympathized with humanity, with the race, with man as man.

What interest have I, says my neighbor, in the people who live on the other side of the globe? I answer, I do not know; not much I fear, or you would not ask the question. But I ask in return: What interest have you in your next door neighbor? Suppose he is starving, what do you care? Suppose his house is on fire, why should you put it out? It is his business, why should you meddle with it? Suppose you see him overboard, why not let him drown? What interest have you in saving his life? But if he dies his wife and children will suffer. What of it? What have you to do with his wife and children? Should I meet a man who would ask such questions as these in earnest, I do not think I should stop to reason with him. I should look upon him as altogether out of my reach.

Every man, unless he is insane, or totally depraved, feels that, somehow, he is under obligation to rescue his neighbor from danger. He may not be able to explain precisely the ground of the obligation, but he cannot well get rid of the conviction that his neighbor has claims upon him. Were he conscious of the ability to rescue him from danger, and should he die through his neglect, he would scarcely be able to avoid a sense of guilt. He might say, I did not kill him, I did not expose him to danger. Was it not his business to take care of himself, and keep out of danger? But the fact that he could have saved him, and did not, would bring remorse with it; and all the world would agree with his conscience and condemn him. Indeed, if you knew that you could save your neighbor's life, and refused to do it, the verdict of mankind would be that you were guilty of his death. You *owe* it to humanity to relieve distress and save life wherever you can. It is precisely in this sense that St. Paul says "he is *debtor* to the Greeks, and to the Barbarians; to the wise, and to the unwise." He felt that all men had claims upon him, which, to the utmost of his ability, he must satisfy or be guilty of their death. Space, distance, cannot modify moral obligation. If we can do it, we are under just as much obligation to save a man on the other side of the globe as on this side, and shall incur just as much guilt for refusing to do so. I have a neighbor who lives within a stone's throw of my own house. His life is threatened. I can save him by stepping to his door, and giving him warning. Of course I am bound to do so. But suppose the same man is in England, and I know that certain parties have taken passage thither on purpose to murder him. I can save him by sending a message upon the Atlantic cable. Am I not under just as much obligation to do it? This obligation to do good to our fellowmen is not a question of distance at all, but of *opportunity.* "*As we have therefore opportunity, let us do good unto all men.*" The Spirit of Christ annihilates space, and inculcates every where the brotherhood of man. I grant that it is more difficult to feel an interest in one you have not seen than in one you have seen. But is it not more manly and noble also? Is it not a glorious thing to be able to see the invisible, and to have a heart as wide as the world; to stand right here, and by our contributions, make the world feel our influence? We ought to accustom ourselves to think of this world, not as a boundless unexplored waste, with no intercourse or sympathy between its different sections, but as it is, a neighborhood, a family united by ten thousand ties of sympathy and interest. John Wesley could say, "My parish is the world." And the world was a great deal larger then than it is now. Steam navigation and the electric telegraph have brought its ends together. Hundreds of years before, one greater than Wesley, when looking out upon the harvest of souls which he came to gather, said, "*The field is the world.*"

The history of mankind has proved that a heart large enough to take in the world cannot beat without shaking the world. This is what we need to-day, the old world-shaking power of Wesley, and Paul, and Christ. Mankind must be redeemed by world-wide hearts. Anything less will not contain the Great Commission which says, "*Go ye into all the world, and preach the Gospel to every creature.*" "My country is the world, mankind are my fellow citizens," is the motto of every true Christian. No man ever grasped that idea with passionate earnestness, who did not move the world. This is the great central idea of Christianity, this is its ruling passion, its all-controlling motive and inspiration, the conquest of the world, in the name of Christ. The more this thought kindles our enthusiasm, the more it permeates all our other thoughts, the more it takes possession of our hearts, the more it enters into all the purposes of our lives, the more it burns and glows within us, the more it drives all the machinery of our being, the more are we in sympathy with Christ. We should be pressed with this thought as with a debt which must be discharged. We should feel it as a burden on our souls, and never should allow ourselves to be happy, except when acting under its inspiration,—*the world*, THE WORLD FOR CHRIST!

We must somehow learn to enter into the circumstances of our fellow men, and feel their wants and woes as though they were our own. We make our missionary contributions as though it were a very indifferent, and common-place affair. We are not enough alive to the tremendous importance of the sublime work in which we are engaged. The greatness of the work ought to exalt our thoughts, and kindle them into a holy and irrepressible activity. We are contributing to the conquest of the whole world; it is for the conversion of twelve hundred millions of souls, multiplied by countless generations yet to come. Christ hath died for them all. It is the body and the blood of the Son of God which we send to the healing of the nations. Who can estimate the value of twelve hundred million souls? We have sometimes felt something of the value of a single soul. With Paul, we have travailed in birth for souls. We have felt that we could sacrifice the last dollar we had on earth to save them. We have felt that this was but the least possible expression of our love for them, that we could die, that we could, with Paul, be "*accursed from Christ for our brethren, our kinsmen according to the flesh.*" In this agony for souls, we have in our measure, entered into Christ's agony. But we feel that we shall never be truly Christ-like, until we can extend this sympathy to the whole world. We want to feel for the whole world, as John Knox did for Scotland, when he prayed, "Give me Scotland or I die." We want to feel as Moses did for Israel, when he cried, "*Oh, this people have sinned a great sin.* * * * *Yet now, if Thou wilt, forgive their sin, and if not, blot me, I pray Thee, out of Thy book which Thou hast written.*"

The more perfectly we become one with the race, the more we become like Christ. If we would be Christ-like, we must, with Him, bear the woes of the world upon our hearts. We must feel that our destiny is bound up with the destiny of the world. We must be willing to sacrifice, and to suffer, even unto death, to save men. Is not this the Spirit of Christ? Are we not to be partakers of Christ's sufferings, as well as co-workers with him, in the salvation of the world? The intimate union between Christ and his church is not, I fear, generally appreciated. The church is the body of Christ, and cannot but be moved by the tremendous heart-throes of sympathy heaving in the unfathomable profound of the Saviour's love. We must, in a manner, enter into his vicarious sacrifice, or we cannot be members of his body. By virtue of our union with Christ, we are partakers of the divine nature, filled with the divine love. Christian hearts are the media through which Christ now manifests his love to the world. "*Let this mind be in you which also was in Christ Jesus, who being in the form of God, took upon him the form of a servant, and became obedient unto death, even the death of the cross.*" What does this mean, but that we should be willing, not only to give of our substance, but to die for the world?

When we are commanded to take up our cross and follow Christ, more is meant than a mere performance of a few easy duties. This command calls us to be partakers of Christ's spirit of sacrifice and suffering love, to a real fellowship in His sufferings for the salvation of the race. If a man would save others, himself he cannot save. "*Except a corn of wheat fall into the ground and die, it abideth alone.*" Just in proportion as a man becomes dead to everything else, he becomes alive to Christ, and a living force in his kingdom. "*If it die it bringeth forth much fruit.*" "*Hereby perceive we the love of God, because He laid down His life for us, and we ought to lay down our lives for the brethren.*" That is, the measure of Christ's love for the world, should be the measure of our love to our fellow men. "*If God so loved us, we ought also to love one another.*" No man, perhaps, ever felt this fellowship with Christ's sacrifice and suffering love more truly than did Paul. "*Always bearing about,*" he says, "*in the body the dying of the Lord Jesus, that the life also of Jesus might be made manifest in our body. For we which live are always delivered unto death for Jesus' sake, that the life also of Jesus might be made manifest in our mortal flesh.*" He even intimates that the sufferings of Christ are not complete without the added sufferings of His disciples. "*Who now rejoice in my sufferings for you, and fill up that which is behind of the afflictions of Christ in my flesh, for His body's sake, which is the church.*" Does not this imply that there is a sense in which we may even be partakers of His vicarious sacrifice? However this may be, it certainly shows that the same spirit which animated Christ, should animate us.

If we are thoroughly baptized into the spirit of Christ, the wretched condition of the mass of mankind will never be out of our minds; it will meet us everywhere. Whenever we read the Bible, we shall remember the millions who never saw it. Whenever we kneel to pray, we shall not forget the millions more that bow down to wood and stone. Whenever we partake of the broken body and shed blood of Jesus, we shall think of the millions who have never heard that precious name, and have received no invitation to this sacred feast. Whenever we hear the Gospel, we shall feel like sending it to earth's remotest bounds. When the knell of death salutes our ears, we shall be reminded that thousands of those who know not Christ are every moment dropping into hell. And we shall have such a sense of the value of these souls as language can never express. I am aware that there are those in the church who will not be able to appreciate what I am now saying. They have never caught the true missionary fire. The conversion of mankind they consider a great work, and very desirable, but it has never become the all-controlling, master passion of their souls. They have endeavored sometimes to compute the value of souls, and see easily enough, that one soul must be worth more than all earthly treasure; but they have never had any such ineffable sense or feeling of its value as I suggest. A true estimate of the value of a human soul is never attained through the ear, or the eye, or any other of the senses, not even through the understanding. It cannot be computed. It defies all mathematical calculation. We have no values like it. It is easy to say that it is a greater work to convert a soul than to conquer an empire, and it is all true; but this gives us no idea of the value of a soul. We may say that all the material universe, though made up of gold and diamonds, weighed against one soul, would be but as the dust in the balance, and this is doubtless also true; but what sense does this give you of the value of a soul? We sometimes say that the blood of Christ is the price of the soul? But the material blood is nothing. It has no value. The value is in that divine agony of love, which gives all efficacy to the blood. We might weigh and measure the blood; but who can measure the agony of the Son of God? Till we can, how shall we estimate the value of the human soul? Souls and material things cannot be compared. As Dr. Whedon would say, they are *incommensurable.* You might as well compare eternity with a steam engine, or a twenty-four gun ship. They are not alike.

They have no points of comparison. Precisely so with all material values and the value of the soul. There are no points of comparison between a soul and a dollar. The value of a soul cannot, therefore, be taught, or communicated from one man to another. It can only be felt. It must be communicated directly to the heart by the Spirit of God.

"*Eye hath not seen, nor ear heard, neither have entered into the heart of man, the things which God hath prepared for them that love him. But God hath revealed them unto us by His Spirit; for the Spirit searcheth all things; yea, the deep things of God. For what man knoweth the things of a man, save the spirit of man which is in him; even so the things of God knoweth no man, but the Spirit of God. Now, we have received not the spirit of the world, but the Spirit which is of God, that we might know the things that are freely given to us of God. Which things also we speak not in the words which man's wisdom teacheth, but which the Holy Ghost teacheth, comparing spiritual things with spiritual. But the natural man receiveth not the things of the Spirit of God, for they are foolishness unto him; neither can he know them, because they are spiritually discerned. But he that is spiritual judgeth all things.*"

"The things which God hath prepared for them that love Him," which "eye hath not seen, nor ear heard, neither have entered into the heart of (the natural) man," give all the value to the soul. If this be so, then are we clearly taught in this passage that the value of the soul is revealed directly by the Spirit, taught by the Holy Ghost, "spiritually discerned." This is the same Spirit, which, when a man is converted, cries out within him, "O my wife, my children, my father, my mother, and all my dear friends, and all the world, O that they might all come to Christ!" Every soul that is born of God, is born into the missionary spirit. It is sometimes quenched very quickly, but all have it at first.

Nothing should be cherished more earnestly, for it is a divine fire, the life of the soul, the noblest gift of God. This is the same spirit which makes a man feel "*Woe is unto me if I preach not the gospel.*" Every minister who is truly called of God, is called in the missionary spirit. This is the same spirit that, when the weight of the world is on the soul, "*maketh intercession for us with groanings which cannot be uttered.*" If you would have this spirit, get near to Christ and you will catch it. Get the baptism of the Holy Ghost, and you will know what it is to feel the value of souls. We contribute for missions upon precisely the same principle that we would save a man from drowning, or rescue him from his burning house, or warn him of threatened danger, or feed him when starving. Millions are starving, threatened, burning, drowning in perdition, and our Master commands, "*Go!*" "Fly to the rescue and save them!" Thousands of godly men start up to obey the command. Shall we sustain them? Shall we defray their expenses? Shall we join with the Master, and say "*Go!*"? How loudly shall we say it? What shall we give this year towards the conversion of the world? The amount of our donations should be graduated somewhat by the magnitude of the work we have to do. Great enterprises require a great outlay of means. If the world is ever converted, it will be through greater sacrifices, and a larger liberality than we have yet seen. This work cannot be overdone. It is a field upon which we can put forth our full strength. If every member of the Christian church should give to the very utmost of his ability, and men full of faith and the Holy Ghost could be found to go, it would take many years to preach the gospel to every creature. Is it not a blessed thought, that here is a field in which our benevolence can have full scope, in which we never can do too much, in which every dollar we can spare can be put directly into the hands of Jesus? How the soul revels in a boundless ocean of benevolent effort! I ask again, how much are we willing to give to Christ this year to send the gospel into all the world, and to every creature? The Methodist church calls for an average of one dollar per member, which in the aggregate amounts to $1,030,978. No person who is not an absolute pauper, ought to pay less than a dollar, while multitudes ought to pay fives, and tens, and twenty-fives, and fifties, and hundreds, and some even thousands every year. If the world is really to be converted, we must begin to lay hold of the business in earnest. It is the great business of the church, and the sooner every member feels it so, the better for the world. As a denomination, our work is but just begun. Methodism in this country is but a hundred years old, and our missionary society less than fifty. How much missionary money do you suppose was paid in the Ohio Conference, embracing at that time the whole of the States of Ohio and Michigan, as well as parts of Kentucky, Virginia, and Indiana in 1820? Bishop Morris, to whom the money was committed by vote of the Conference, for the purpose of sending it forward to the Parent Society, informs us that the entire aggregate of all the collections amounted to *nineteen dollars and a fraction over!* Last year (1865-6) Ohio and Michigan alone gave $78,562. The entire amount contributed by the whole church in the same year, (1820)) was $823. The amount contributed last year, (1865-6) was $671,090. A very respectable advance certainly, though I think you will all agree with me, that it is far less than it ought to be, when you consider that this amounts to an average of only seventy-seven cents per member. But this standard has been raised by slow degrees. In 1820 we gave an average of three mills per member; in 1825, one cent, one mill; in 1830, two cents, seven mills; in 1835, four cents, six mills; in 1840, eighteen cents, seven mills;

in 1845, eight cents, seven mills; in 1850, fifteen cents, six mills; in 1855, twenty-five cents, five mills; in 1860, twenty-five cents; in 1865, seventy-eight cents, one mill, the highest average yet attained. It is humiliating to know that our own Conference has never reached a higher standard than sixty-two cents per member, and still more humiliating that last year (1865-6) we should fall down to fifty-six cents per member. Are we so much poorer than our sister Conferences as to make this necessary? Will missions supported at such a rate ever convert the world? We must nearly double our collections this year, to do our share in meeting our current missionary appropriations. Last year (1865-6) we raised less than nine thousand dollars, this year the work demands fifteen thousand.*

If our people understood the magnitude, and grandeur, and infinite importance of this work, who can believe that they would hesitate to furnish the funds required? We are abundantly able. Let us run over our field, and see if, in Christian consistency, we can afford to do less. The church is asked to sustain ten missionaries among the Indians, at an expense of $4,600. Is this too much? We are enjoying their hunting grounds, and as the wave of civilization rolls on, they must be submerged. Can we do less as they go down, than to point them to the Saviour, and through him to fairer hunting grounds on high? Our Indian wars, we are told, are costing us now a million of dollars a week. Every Indian we kill and send to perdition, costs us hundreds of thousands of dollars. Would it not be better to send less gun powder and whisky, and more missionaries among them? One hundredth part of the outlay of means, with correspond-

* NOTE.—We are pained to learn from the report of the treasurer of our Conference Missionary Society, made since the above was written, that we have raised during the year just closed, only about one-half the amount apportioned to us. Shall this be so in the year to come?

ing missionary efforts, would save all this effusion of blood, and instead of thrusting them in all their savageness down to hell, would raise multitudes of holy spirits to the skies. Has Christianity nothing for savages but the sword? If the nation pays a million dollars a week to kill these children of the forest, is it too much for a great church like ours to pay $4,600 a year to save them? O that the sword of the Spirit were the sword of the nation, how much less of blood and treasure would our warfare cost, and how much more certain and glorious our triumph!

Next we turn to Africa; ravaged, plundered, degraded Africa, once the great luminary of the ancient world, now, in every sense, the darkest and most wretched quarter of the globe. But if I read the signs of the times aright, the star of Africa is again in the ascendant, that darkest hour which precedes the day is past, and the Sun of Righteousness is about to arise upon that benighted land with healing in his wings. That the Christian religion, and especially that form of it called Methodism, is adapted to the African mind, has been sufficiently demonstrated in this country. No race ever proved more susceptible to its holy influences. Our missionary work in Africa began in the right spirit to succeed. When Melville B. Cox, our first missionary to Africa, was warned that if he went to that country, he soon must die, he replied, "I know I cannot live long in Africa, but I hope to live long enough to get there, and if God please that my bones shall lie in an African grave, I shall have established such a bond between Africa and the church at home, as shall not be broken until Africa is redeemed." Thus he went, and laid down his life for that country, and dying, said, "Let a thousand fall, but let not Africa be given up." Shall not we respond to his sainted spirit? It shall not be given up. The church will not give it up. God will not give it up. Africa shall be redeemed. Had we the spirit of this Christian hero, how much should we be willing to contribute towards the redemption of Africa to-day? The church confines her operations to Liberia, and is asked for only $15,400 to sustain twenty-eight missionaries. Ought we not to do more? Ought we not to expend hundreds of thousands in evangelizing the natives of that land? Men adapted to that work are being educated in this country to-day by the thousand. Let us pray the Lord of the harvest to send forth laborers into His harvest, and that the mantle of Melville B. Cox may fall upon the sons of Africa, that they may return by multitudes to proclaim the unsearchable riches of Christ in their fatherland. We want money for Africa, but we want the self-sacrificing zeal of the first martyr to this mission more. Let us turn from Africa to Asia, the cradle of the world. How much shall we give for the conversion of China? This mission never was so prosperous as now. The work here has thus far been chiefly a work of preparation. We had the language to acquire, a Christian literature to create, chapels and parsonages to erect, native helpers to secure, and a church to organize. But now we have gained a foothold in this vast empire; we have but to prosecute our labors with becoming vigor to achieve the most sublime results. We have now five missionaries, seven assistant female missionaries, and thirty-six native helpers; in all forty-eight missionaries in this field. Two more missionary families are on their way to reinforce them. There have been issued from our press in China during the past year, almost ten million of pages, (9,937,000) including the entire New Testament, and the book of Proverbs, with tracts and other matter indispensable to the prosecution of our work. To carry forward this work the church is asked for $20,344. This is the outlay we propose to make this year towards the conversion of the most populous empire on the globe, an empire in which ten thousand missionaries might be employed to advantage. Is it too much? Is it enough? Let your contributions for China answer.

And then we turn to India. This is, at present, the most prosperous and promising of all our foreign missions. The people are every where accessible, throng by multitudes to our missionaries, and hear with eagerness; many are being converted, and native preachers and helpers are being rapidly raised up. As a church, we have become responsible for ten millions of people in the part of India we occupy, pledging ourselves to cultivate this field, with the understanding that it is to be left to us by other denominations. Here we have founded a Christian College, and have a regularly organized Methodist Conference, with (including one hundred and thirty-five school teachers, and forty-four native preachers and exhorters) a force of two hundred and fourteen missionaries. No portion of our work is crying more loudly for reinforcements from home. Rev. E. W. Parker, P. E., of Moradabad District, closes his report by saying, "Remember that our mission stations are, on an average, fifty miles apart, and that each station represents a population of five hundred thousand souls, and yet most of these stations have but one missionary each. What we ask and plead for now is, that our church may send us men enough to supply all our large stations with two missionaries each. Is it too much to ask that we may have two men for five hundred thousand souls? Let the church send forth her men and means, accompanied by her earnest prayers, and ere another century shall pass away, the Methodist church will have accomplished in India, a work such as has been done in America during the century past." Should the church do her duty, this will be considered a very tame prophecy in fifty years from to-day. For this vast work there is demanded this year, $46,924, not a half a cent a soul for all these starving millions we are pledged to feed. In view of the great Sacrifice of Christ we ask, is this enough? You may ask if these missions do anything towards supporting themselves. O yes; India contributed twenty-two thousand dollars towards the expenses of the mission last year, nearly half as much as the appropriation in 1867. It is said that God helps those that help themselves. Let us do likewise. And now we turn to Europe.

In Europe our missions are in Bulgaria, (Turkey) Germany and Scandinavia. To sustain our work in Bulgaria, where we have three missionaries, the church asks for $4,112. Facilities for the enlargement of this work are increasing every day, and three more missionaries are called for, but cannot be sent at present for the want of funds.

In Germany we have a regularly organized Conference, with fifty-eight missionaries, a Theological Seminary, and a Publishing House. The amount asked for all the purposes of this great and prosperous mission is $34,884. The church is indebted to no part of the modern world more than to Germany. It is probably, to-day exerting more influence upon the religious thought of mankind than any other nation. A denomination expecting to exert anything like a general influence in the grand movement to convert the world, which is now being inaugurated, must take Germany in its programme, as one base of operations of vast strategetical importance. German thought rectified, and fired by the Holy Ghost, is a magazine of power, such as can be found nowhere else in this world. Of this we are availing ourselves in the most effectual way through our mission in Germany. The day is not far distant, when our Nasts, and Warrens, and Hursts will be the great lights in our denominational horizon. German thought filtered through sanctified Anglo-American mind will make the richest and purest theological literature in the world. I look for great treasures in our denominational literature from this source. Not only is this the land of Luther, and the Reformation, but we must not forget that Wesley himself received his best instruction in the great practical truths of our religion, justification by faith, the witness of the Spirit, and entire satisfaction, from the same country, nor that the founders of our church, Mrs. Heck and Phillip Embury, were Germans. We are but paying a debt we owe, in endeavoring to rekindle in Germany the old fire from heaven, which has been smothered by the dull formality, and often undisguised infidelity of a State religion. Methodism is to do precisely the same work for Germany which it has done for England and the United States, not only gather a powerful membership into its own fold, but quicken and vitalize the older churches.

In Scandinavia we have twenty-one missionaries supported by an appropriation of $15,545. This mission has been blessed with considerable success, and in Copenhagen we have one of the finest Methodist churches in the world. But two thirds of the converts of this mission come to America. The master builder of our church in Copenhagen, laid the foundation of Heck Hall, and his son is studying for the ministry in the Northwestern University. Many of the Scandinavian workmen were converted during the building of this memorial edifice. It was my happinness to meet with them in the chapel of the University, and to witness great demonstrations of spiritual power among them. The reflex influence of our German and Scandinavian work in Europe upon the same work in this country, is very great. Our missionaries act undesignedly, and in spite of themselves, as a sort of colonization agents, and send their converts to build up American churches, instead of keeping them to strengthen their own. But the gain to the kingdom of Christ is the same, and we need all the good foreign elements we can have in this country to counteract the influence of the bad. How much shall we give for our missions in Europe, for Bulgaria, Germany and Scandinavia?

From Europe we turn to South America. Here we have nine missionaries. We have been compelled to make an appropriation for church building at Buenos Ayres this year, which materially increases the amount expended in this field. For years our work in this mission remained almost stationary, but latterly, new doors are opening before us in almost every direction. Were we able to move promptly and strongly, we might, without doubt, in a very short time, greatly advance the interests of Christ's kingdom, especially in the Argentine Republic. We ought to expend, if we could command the money, $150,000 per year for some years to come, to establish schools and churches, and maintain missionaries in this Southern half of our continent. This year the church is asked for $43,650. Will any one who knows anything of the extent and character of South America say that this is enough? It should be remembered that we have no Church Extension Society for our foreign field, and that the foregoing appropriations are designed to aid in the building of churches and parsonages, as well as to pay the salaries of the missionaries. When this is taken into account, it will be seen that our foreign missions are conducted upon the most rigid principles of economy. This closes the list of our foreign missions, not one of which do we work up to one-tenth of our attainable power. Who can doubt, if we felt the value of souls as we ought, and were making the propagation of Christ's kingdom the great work of our lives, but we could, as a church, give an average of ten dollars each per year, to convert the world? Do we not lay more than that year by year unnecessarily upon the altar of fashion and pride? Do we not expend more than that in useless, not to say sinful, luxuries? It was many years ago, when we were not as strong as we are now, that Dr. Olin said, "Our proportionable share of the work of converting the world, gives us a hundred million of immortal men to our watch-care and tender mercies." To-day then, more than a hundred million starving men have a right to look to us for the bread of life. More than a hundred million souls, for whom Christ died, are dependent upon us for a knowledge of the way of salvation. They are our charge. Their blood will be required at our hands. Shall they perish without the offer of salvation through our neglect? Millions of them must, unless the zeal and the liberality of the church can be increased. If there is any truth in the Bible, all idolaters are excluded from the kingdom of heaven, the nations that forget God, the great mass of the heathen, are turned into hell. The church holds the keys of the kingdom of heaven, and will not open to them. There is not the least doubt but millions of souls go down to hell every year through the criminal parsimony, and indifference of the church. We try to get rid of this tremendous responsibility, and comfort ourselves in our indifference and illiberality by such passages as these: "*In every nation he that feareth God, and worketh righteousness, is accepted with Him.*"

"*When the Gentiles, which have not the law, do by nature the things contained in the law, these having not the law, are a law unto themselves.*" But the most these passages teach, is that the salvation of a heathen is not absolutely impossible. There may be here and there a Socrates, who in spite of adverse circumstances will be saved. So a saint may grow up in a brothel, but for one such instance, you will find a thousand in Christian families. So you will find a thousand saved under a Christian civilization, where you will find one in heathendom. The truth remains the same, that millions go down to perdition for the want of the bread of life which we withhold. Could the whole church be brought to feel this overwhelming truth, there would be no rest until the gospel should be preached in all the world and to every creature, but not every man can bear all the world upon his heart at once. The field of vision is too wide for many near-sighted mortals. They cannot comprehend it. It requires a degree of intelligence, as well as piety, to which every man has not attained. We have to grow to this by degrees as we do to anything else. But we now come to a field which no man can fail to comprehend. I refer to what are called our Domestic Missions. 1st. To foreign populations in the United States, Welsh, German, Scandinavian, and Chinese, for which the church is asked to contribute $64,350. 2d. To our English speaking people on our frontiers, in the heathen districts of our great cities, and in the South, for which there are appropriated $575,354, Thus, $639,704 are appropriated to our domestic work. This seems like a large sum, and so it is; but in all soberness, I am compelled to say, from what I know of the work, that it is not one-half as much as we need. Every department of this work is of the utmost importance to us, not only as a church, but as a nation. Godless, infidel, and even idolatrous foreigners are pouring into this country by the hundred thousand. They threaten not only our faith, but our noblest institutions, and our most righteous laws. We must Christianize them, or they will demoralize, infidelize and heathenize us. I have said that the reflex influence of our missionary work in Germany and Scandinavia is very great upon the same class of work in this country, and I may add, *vice versa*, the influence of the German and Scandinavian work in this country is still greater upon the fatherland of these peoples. Thousands of letters are written home every year by those who have found both liberty and religion in this happy land. Each one of these letters is read by at least a half a score of persons. Sanctified by friendship and kinship, and a thousand fond recollections of former days, who can tell the effect of these messages of love, upon the hearts of the dear ones at home? Every such letter is as good as a sermon, and worth a score of religious tracts. These pleasant echoes from a far-off land go before our missionaries, and prepare thousands of hearts for the "*good seed.*" This greatly enhances the importance of the work among our foreign population.

Then the importance of our work in the Territories, in the newer portions of the Western States, and in the heathen districts of our great cities cannot be over-estimated. The gospel alone can rescue our new territories from anarchy, mob law and barbarism. We must follow the early settlers, and lay the foundation of a Christian civilization among them. There are no missionaries more self-sacrificing and laborious, than the men who do this work. There are none whose labors yield a more fruitful harvest. No other class of missionaries are as a rule, so poorly supported. When representatives of other denominations, do venture to stand by our side at the front, they are always better supported than we are. If any one supposes the heroic days of Methodism are over, let him ask the bishop to send him to one of the very best of these frontier appointments. If that does not satisfy him, let him ask to be transferred to the Southern States, and districts covering whole States, circuits two hundred miles long, insults, threats suggestive of pistol shots and halters, coarse fare, and abundance of hard work, will probably be satisfactory.

This brings me to speak of the vast importance of our Southern work.

The four million slaves that have just been born to freedom and clothed with all the rights of citizenship have sometimes been called the wards of the nation. If they are the wards of the nation, they certainly ought to be the children of the church. Like children, they need education and discipline to prepare them for their new duties and responsibilities. There are no other four million human beings on earth who are so ignorant, and who at the same time are so eager to learn. There are none who more readily embrace the Christian religion. They are the heathen at our doors, the man fallen among thieves, the Lazarus at our gate, with, hitherto, not even the dogs for their friends. They know our agency in their emancipation, and have that confidence in us which makes the gospel a welcome message at our hands. Our success among them has thus far been very great. The re-construction of the rebel states upon an anti-slavery basis will give us great influence with the governing class of southern society, for our record will bear the test of time, and the longer it stands the brighter it will grow, while that of the pro-slavery and disloyal churches will become more and more infamous as the spirit of the age flows in upon the South, and the principles of freedom and justice prevail.

At the last session of the Mission Committee some doubt was expressed as to whether the Government would protect us in our rights in this field. But that question has happily been settled by a patriotic Congress, and henceforth the Southern States are free to us. We are becoming so thoroughly entrenched there that it will soon be impossible for any power to dislodge us without driving the nation to arms again. Should an attempt be made to drive us out, half a million bristling bayonets would rise as by magic to defend us. Methodism is henceforth to be a power in this Government. No element entering into the re-construction of the nation is of more importance than the influence of our missions in the South. God helping us, we will forge bands of union for this nation, which all the powers of darkness can never burst asunder. Three years ago we had scarcely a foothold in all the South.

Now in Mississippi and Louisiana we have a Conference with some thirty ministers, eight thousand members, $100,-000 in Church property, a Theological Seminary and a weekly church paper in New Orleans. In Texas, also, we have a Conference with more than twenty preachers, and some two thousand members. In South Carolina, likewise, we have a Conference with more than twenty ministers, and a membership of six thousand, with a weekly religious paper and a Biblical Institute at Charleston. Also in Virginia and North Carolina we have a Conference with some sixteen preachers, the number of membership I do not know. We have two Conferences in Tennessee—the Holston and the Tennessee. The Holston Conference, situated in East Tennessee, comprises about twenty thousand members, one hundred and thirty seven local preachers, and fifty-one traveling ministers. The Tennessee Conference, situated in the western part of the State, comprises some thirty-five traveling ministers, forty-nine local preachers, and three thousand members. In West Georgia and Alabama, as the result of seventeen months' effort ending July 1st, 1867, we have eighty-eight traveling and one hundred and twenty-five local preachers, eighty-three church buildings, one hundred and fifty-six Sunday schools, with five hundred and fifty-nine officers and teachers, and seven thousand scholars. During seventeen months eleven thousand and forty-two persons in that field have united with the M. E. Church. This field is about to be organized into two Conferences. The Missouri, Arkansas and Kentucky Conferences have been greatly prospered since the war.

Who doubts that a million of dollars in Methodist mission churches and schools, could be expended to advantage in the South the coming year? No better investment could be made for the church or the nation, than thus to appropriate a million of dollars annually for ten years to come. Patriotism, benevolence and piety, all plead with one voice for the prosecution of this work. If we would establish a common civilization, and perpetuate the peace and unity of the nation, if we would help not only those that need help, but those who, in this country, need it most, and save the souls of the perishing, where they are most ready to come to Christ, let us in the name of God and liberty, to the utmost of our ability, push our missions in the South. Thus our line of battle extends to every quarter of the globe, and we must fight it out upon this line, if it takes us to the day of judgment. Hitherto we have only sent out skirmishers, to feel of the enemy, and ascertain his position. Shall we call them in, or will the main army move forward to sustain them? Methinks I see the Captain of our salvation waving his sceptre over this grand army; and flinging the blood-stained banner of the cross to the breeze, he cries, FORWARD! MARCH!

Let the command go down through all the ranks of the great army of God, and with firm and steady tread, keeping step to the music of the gospel, let us make our charge upon Paganism among our Indians, upon Fetichism in Africa, upon the Boodhism and Brahmanism of China and India, upon the Mohammedism of Turkey, upon the formalism and infidelity of Germany and Scandinavia, upon the Romanism of South America, and upon the kingdom of Satan generally, in our Southern States, and in our midst. Let us charge unitedly, promptly, generously, heroically, and for the love of Christ. What do you say brethren? Shall we fail for the want of supplies? What are you willing to do for the conquest of the world, in the name of Christ? Let your Missionary offerings answer. When the battle is over, and the victory is won, we shall all pass in review before Him that cometh in the clouds of heaven, with power and great glory. May our deeds be such as we shall rejoice to have rehearsed before an assembled universe!—AMEN.

www.ingramcontent.com/pod-product-compliance
Lightning Source LLC
LaVergne TN
LVHW011139110826
845150LV00008B/2409

* 9 7 8 1 4 1 8 1 9 3 4 7 8 *